D1440834

# MANIFEST

Cynthia Arrieu-King

**SWITCHBACK BOOKS**
CHICAGO

Copyright © 2013 Cynthia Arrieu-King. All rights reserved.
No part of this book may be reproduced without the permission of the publisher.

ISBN-13: 978-0-9786172-8-8
ISBN-10: 0978617282

Library of Congress Control Number: 2013930784

Book design: Elle Collins
Cover art and design: Britannie Bond

Switchback Books
Hanna Andrews, Editor
S. Whitney Holmes, Editor
Colleen O'Connor, Managing Editor
editors@switchbackbooks.com
www.switchbackbooks.com

*To my family*

# TABLE OF CONTENTS

*You still don't have a face.*
 –Alice Notley

## ODE TO NOT DREAMING

I told you wildness is hands-off. When asleep,
that darling space saves her lunch dollar in a jar.
Over a week, and falling asleep to another chance Eiffel Tower,
a girl can still love and run to climb that height eight times.
She ignores everything but something golden that lights up.
Diesel wipes a face. Wildness existing in a lens, rampant
in our cells. This sleepy lung of smoke
drawn by hand, a hand reaching into this dream
so real it looks original or yours. It's a thin glass
over an egg shaded and shaded in terminal thoughts.
I think: Who knows what aspects of dreams and reality
run down orange halls in a parallel sense?
Slow gold licks all the windows.

The green glass of your eyes teems with birds,
twin wings inexplicable as paste. In this art,
each ordinary mosaic separates to single shells, rouge
or Cerulean, the how-pretty inlaid panels and a brooch
of distraction. Mom and the Empire Era Secretary
stare each other down in the museum foyer. That trembling gilt
split by wood still, still holding. A man stands nearby and
coughs. His eyes and what I don't say: beauty.
Not knowing. Our happy prisms vague prisons,
the curtain odd. No thought lies across a sweet pink
museum scratched and lethal in actual streets. Rubbed white,
I hold your sleeve. A dream comes out of your eyes and mouth.

The war wears rubber shoes to hide its feet. And after the splash,
what is it about this nightmare that makes me so speechless?
That makes the mind reach for cover under something plastic
and unseen. That blood, it isn't dreamed. A mind filters
fickle and preserving, and always a bloodied sun bursts
under damp quilts. Oil wells, your sparkle is a distant conflagration.
Then, finding the right distance to stand from an image
to see what face is hidden in its nickel shreds—a step forward,
two steps back—you use restraint for tying nightmare's hands behind.

A museum hall breaks into the past. I'm impressed
with a medieval room, tapestries that calm Mom. Her bones
shrank from being a girl in war, bone soaps shrinking in flesh foam.
She hates unidentifiable wax and avant and foil flowers. Pressure
from the meaning of *dominant* and *when*. Burying seedling
guilt, my eyes confused about who was saying and knowing:
what proved failure. No concepts strung together haphazard feel like
a solid rail in the world. Even yesterday, my mother stood
in front of a chic gigantic mural, paint peeling on a German building,
white wings revealing hot bare brick. Texture
of do-nothing. Pretty decay. She wasn't impressed by that nor
by an arrangement of Lucite cubes glued to a wall in a cloud.

Don't go back to sleep, I say to a knock on the door.
But after a long period of being pale, I get curious again,
vital and happy—stillness being the only thing that makes
drawn, grey water tip out clean. To rest, okay, but look.
The flaw is doom touched to you with a waxen hand
while you sleep. Underneath this comfortable dream
lie cold tiles, real tiles, and a stranger debate: a lost man argues
his dog's tail needs to be cut in the middle: *He licks it. Cut it short.*
A vet says that won't help since the problem was the itch in
the dog's rectum. That's why he licks. She says, *Wouldn't it be better*
*to solve this with medicine rather than cutting the tail in two?*
*No*, he says, leaning forward. *No, no. You need to cut the tail in two.*

## SELF-PORTRAIT: LOOKING AND LOOKING AWAY

Who needs a cartographer for wrinkles?
So far, free-floating fucked-up worry
is no gun, is all pose-less ire
in quite a cheap cup.

Imagining your lips to see what face I make—
always up—brilliant mouth of gold jelly.
A shadow dragging a sweater of longing. Snap.

Here, lengths of icicles flash whiteness.
I aimed to represent this face khaki—
khaki on black, photographed gazing at you
or gazing inward at an abstract you
                              until I squander the thought—

                              and struggle with this room, framed—

## HOW DO YOU DEFINE BLISS, LOVE?

What emerges from the hectic, contagious public
is a code that could sound foreign if you took a break.
The birds all trying to sing *freedom* and *beauty*
are risks that need a hideout. Bliss is not knowing,
is the hedge trimmed right above eye level.
I thought about knocking on your door but left
like a cat that smacks into the door jamb, and
plays it off, licking his paw; I pet the neighbor's dog.
Why do I want everything to glom together? Why
do I need again a small steel pair of scissors to
cut through me? I don't mean as if, filed separately,
we can keep life to ourselves. There
are a million beauties I'd hoard for you.
Keep them secret and snug down, this war
of hiding out in our own heads and mugging.

I know. I could barely sneak beauty into my pants.
Alice had a set of teeth like a string of pearls, harder
to hide, and attracting kisses. Tim across the street
might wake up fog-free and pink-cheeked. Beauty
as camo, shrubs to carry on our heads. Groceries,
a schedule—we were all thinking about the mother past
and tried to protect it by loosening the cords.
But knowing is bliss, too. You break out
an emerald velvet sack and dump it out:
diamond questions. Can a soul be cut?
Are you screwed if yours is? Where are all
the people who made me think I waited, bright
as glaring roof, copper and tall, who proved
my longer thoughts had something to them?
That's what happiness is. Knowing surrounded by not knowing.

## WABISABI, NEBRASKA

Flying over farm circuitry, interlocked pools and trees,

landscape that belonged to no one, belongs to no one,

earthenware with flaws bunched through it,

happenstance avenues and

waiting for the lavatory door to accordion open, I watched

all the razed corn under the road grid.

That door buckled for a good three minutes. Lock not thrown,

a pause like those egg films when

an un-hatched chick presses against cracked membrane and shell

dome shifting, breathing and wobbling,

the lock started to bust through the plastic. I thought

a child stuck in there, but it was a man who burst out looking

down—my trying to slide open the lock

from outside hadn't worked—and stepping onto the jet,

he jangled a zigzag from his hand, black plastic that snapped into a cane.

What flies apart:

doors, happenstance, a fastener flying off—

the incomplete, the impermanent, imperfect and wilder besides:

remember you and I, we'd howled at the woman

clearly worse after her TV makeover, post machine-of-powders,

her big reveal topped with golden sombrero—sequins really

bring out the glint in dental fillings—

and flying over farm, city, silo filigree, without her knowing,

I think of her before-face, quiet and pale,

a landscape that belonged to no one, belongs to no one.

## L'ASSEMBLÉE NATIONALE

It hung in my mind, a cloud of promising metallic qualities.
A metal frame stretched out, an umbrella's skeleton flared
to introduce suction and assemblage: women
at work on truths untied and forever reframed
with perpetual interruption. Cascading green velvet
and chocolate thread. Moreover, stares cruising past,
walk signals on and blinking.

A student walked in and asked the boss if I—and not the others—
would teach her to scan a heart all morning. Ultrasound it.
*Of course*, I said, right
as a doctor stood outside the boss' door
to say she disliked
a too-bright quality in my work.

In a dark lab, I leaned my hand on top of the student's
and showed her that her death grip on the probe
kept the camera tucked firmly under the fourth rib
and would never focus a good picture for her. Heart windows diverse,
she had to sweep the wand over a patient's ribs—
like a gaze ranging a whole store
for a walk identifiable
in lack
of loping, or side to side,
its person wearing known khakis, slow toss of hair.

When she was four,
my mother crawled, a secret,
down one arrondissement, across a bridge,
knees down another cobblestone mile,
Germans sniping from the top of L'Assemblée Nationale,
the largest building downtown.

Thunder roll of bombardment or not, her mother crawled above her,
mother an arms and legs shelter.

*That's enough,*
she never said to little me.
*That's enough, stop looking in the tin*
at a stack of identical sweets.
She knew one day I'd learn my own enough

and gaze—a bright *enough*—would fill the space
around each fog, brick, and soft face arriving.

When language throws out the last
heel of bread, failing to break your purpose;
when speechless, I've likely seen a brand of mother—say,
a many-faced Picasso—red, framed, grandly lit, and known
beyond the hundred sweating heads—

her white mask, each disfigured eye stuck wild
on a green drift means the mother leaving, her child
quiet behind a door, human instinct on her many lips,

crimsons burning the stillest face.

# EXPLAINING THE SUBLIME

She says yes trillium is like morning glories but with three long leaves,
much better colors. Not so biological, I say. She

pictures rolling hills, crocuses, and apple blossoms
swooning, perfumed. I say, no your brain is parsing that beauty,
more like huge mountains or vistas of the sea
so blunt
      or featureless they're terrifying.
      Fear of the unknown, all that water making you feel small.

But how can a waterfall make you afraid? she asks.

                      Like you look
into a canyon and a handful of pearls drops
through your chest, I say.

She blinks. I spread my arms out:
Extreme love, when you're scared by how much you love someone.

She says, I've not experienced that yet.

So I go retrograde, or long as in an involved classroom discussion,
to explain fear of the sublime
to the girl who missed weeks
because a doctor misdiagnosed her with cancer.

## INTO THE CELERY DOORS

Around the bodega, its blunt black awning,

alstroemeria, ronunculi trimmed to the ankle,

you take a quick break from make-believe blue

blossoms to sandwiches on carts. A bus horn

and a busker's song braid inside refreshing bliss.

A white splotch hangs above emptiness. Iron scent

touches the ticket edge before you run downstairs:

the dream of monotony gone, heads ascending

to some nightish above. Those maybes light pink signals,

a cardiology afloat over the wide whiteness,

cabs cabbed. Do you love the square

or sinking into bed more? It's hard to say.

A cool green gate to pass under, a cool green pill

and bliss—your affection for waiting for 2 AM trains,

your goods wrapped in yesterday's *Times*. A bamboo grove

of guesses: Should I be on this side, or the other?

And your hair blows back in gratitude for the violin screech,

a shapeless bit of light swimming to you through black.

The word *city* opens its silver robe like a stick of gum. Let it.

## DEER OF LOS ANGELES

They overhear but don't understand
a man moving his mouth:
*I'm writing a script about*
*a girl who's afraid of cars!*

A Mercury Cougar glazes past, red, and parks.
They touch their noses to convertible hoods.

Who will give them a hamburger today?
What car will they leap,
                    brown-fixed, these deer farouche—
        spray-painted flanks—necks tagged by scraping past?

Bloated deer wait, overhear an egregious mistake.
They read carefully
how to deal with broken glass, star maps,
fur matted with mayonnaise:
                    one rotates an ear, stiff, toward a window
                    *listen to him smell him*
                    a boy like a dead foot.

Trust and day-long fear.
Every moment is danger, every bullet a woman.

To deer there's no *bride catches on fire*, is there?

Deer dart away, big hairy words
like *freedom* and *will*,
two words wearing sunny lamé while
junked-out kids not making it big
chat, quiz each other on their first memories,

actually thinking
*I can fly* and jumping off the garage roof.

Paper dries and blows past deer dry and blank.
As if their broken interest could kick in your skull for that anthem.

Blasphemy requires this one be dead serious:
the deer touch their noses to the convertible hoods.

Parking lot so crowded with cars late to school,
three deer actually puzzle and slide between
bumpers, stand behind a car a woman backs
downhill. She brakes
                    at the sight of their bulk. Rearview tan fur.

She half rants and gets out.

One looks uphill. Another's
leg barely touches the bumper.
Thirteen minutes. Thirteen

minutes standing with these
tame deer who don't
speak English or flinch, slowly becoming men.

## SETSUKO HARA

A bristling fir
whispered about my vanishing. The great silence.

How, fade to black,
I, the girl of your dreams, am also this tan middle-aged man
I swept into suits
and hanged. No marriage, your Eternal Virgin
in black and white. Black
and white flips a skirt, a frown until I, so famous,
fly like a buck into woods no one can see.

They knock. *I don't live here*, I say.
I keep the cedar door to.

Here in the house, a moth bats
a lantern, holding to a flame-opulent scrim.

Slatted sandals. This clatter of plums—
I'm a chime films end with
after twenty years of poses,
striding into the fake hall as you wanted,
tilting my head
to a crinoline kimono. Catapulted to billboards
glutting the seashore, I lived this thought:

No one's going to burn my bones
until smoke stops its creep from the kettle.
No smoked femur of mine will
mix water.

A wash to paint a portrait of sad ether,
a black to give the impression of bottomless eyes
filled with whatever you
wanted.

The blunt kite
of appearing, and now I shade the hanging wash,
my hand
a visor, my hand breaks up old ash.

The sun an unexpected hand.
I say behind the door,
*She doesn't live here.*

It's been years since I tired, tiptoeing for light meters.
The fecund night of other people's feelings.
And now I hide,
a black LP played in perpetuity.

I brush the air unseen. Is life disappointing?

Yes.

Kurosawa. Ozu. Narusa. Inagaki.
Go on, claim with all names,
grab noise at sea, and unplanned sea foam chilling my calves
for the twenty-third time. You can't
film this yourself. Out there
withers millions of me in celluloid.
I accepted your fifty-cent tickets—

that hardly assuaged
my brother struck by a train before my eyes,
hardly your tripod,
my face gone among chrysanthemums
and today,
a long still of myself:

radishes in rain.
Oyster-dumb, not hoping for grit or a pearl.

I feel your undying admiration,
tiny boxes of white cream on spoons.

Snow lands on everything you knew of me.
Snow beyond a dry indigo curtain,
this backwards, unseen breath.
Into a kettle's voice I disappear,

a smile useless without a fence.

My heart thuds
an all-interior vista
almost big
as what you loved so much, the idea
of this steady sea, these happy eyes.

## CAKE KISSED

Hello sponge, sweet map of my hand. Oven quarters—
that black solitary. Hardly a way to cut through things.
Nothing to do: fondly exist, all brisk pleasures
like a nutmeg fume of mood. Too, part of this good
is disproportionate. A fond, if ironic dream.
In gold cashmere, five brisk measures, a leisure
at other times the better claim, a quiet map:
how you rub the fat in matters. To sit, a hot
dark hour easier to pass as a fix, a correct shipwreck.

Foam risen. Exactly what I mean when I talk this fond
if ironic dream. Soul, we let you bake a little. And renounce
grains and membranes to enter a life of kitchens, office
creatures, the unexpressed. Into the words we can bake
a little "a." A cake is kissed.  A good wait is.

## JE EST UN AUTRE

All I notice and love are abstruse curtains of light across corners
or my shoulder pushing against a blue door.

I don't know why my brain burns, thinks of one thing,
how my life has been arranged by both myself and

quick alien gentry that are the universe the sunlight hurts
so that only by keeping quiet can I maintain sufficient

turgor pressure. Water a dying plant and see it whiff up:
my naps more frequent. A slap on the wrist, the warning I

should speak more at my own party so my friend won't be stranded
with friends he doesn't know. It slaked brutal

and quiet at the table laden with green and orange salads.
In my mind it was like or almost like diving into air

with questions, forced tap dancing, shucking and jiving about Neal's
window job, throe of anecdote, bystanders agree *girls on craigslist rule;*

*they screw you and leave,* a field, pleasantly            (silence)


O needless strings of

simile dangling from a hook
I'll never reach. No, I don't like trying to think what's wrong with me.

Even golden calves know better than to talk out their
moos or what golden hope at the center of all went bad

and let conversation with even you, beautiful girl, lance such pins
into my heart. Well. I'll wait here until a new thing comes—

trick of season, of love that regular leaves dry without. The shindig
of which I never speak. Oh fuck. Here come the k sounds, the long a's.

# FRENCH MOTHER WITH TORNADO SIRENS IN BACKGROUND

I don't know why I was such a dog for all of you.

It was misty. From the lookout
I could see the other state from this
state.

Give me a real dog.

I wasn't yet a mother who put her things in a trunk
and sailed three weeks
to the states.

The Seine carried away my paper sack,
two small tin dogs
painted red,
and my snack:
jam and toast
drowned in a tunnel
of dusk-charged air.

It was misty. From the lookout
I could see the other state from this
state:

the world goes by and the world goes by me.

The Ohio rolled brown and full of tin caps
I couldn't pluck
and bag. I wait.
I've got a clear throat and
no pumice
can mend this.

My son's hat, white and whisked
into the Charles.

The Hudson full of boats
wind swept past
and tipped. We baked,
a sun scouring down like we were dirt,
wind over my hair.

I know how George crossed the Delaware
whereas I
to get my points across
have used bridges,

my skirt dipped black into the pond, Le Jardin des Tuileries.

No thought-of-the-day
for all the lonely.

## [THE PROCEDURE REMAINED WHOLLY MYSTERIOUS TO ME]

The procedure remained wholly mysterious to me and I could not

say *buckle*, say *the shine of patent leather shoes.*

I half shut my eyes, hoping to hear my language the way

a foreigner would hear it:

a roundness of red, the roundness of carnations—

*geese* and *fray*, *tenor* and *fall*—

how holy things descend in the order of appearance:

*vote* fades to blips, a tile floor goes ulcerous, a dress-shirt

limp with the tide pools. Whatever remains mid-verse

sleeps with both eyes closed to exact a series of desserts and club sandwiches:

glassy lemon pies, the red slash,

that particular angle of smile frosts the face, bends the mirror

through representational sadness and from the swirled green

beneath every painting, there is a snow boat for

traveling away from here: avocado ellipses,

a green brown smear

and flat

beneath every canvas, alone hatches its eggs.

## [NO LITERAL FIELD OF BLACK MOOD COULD SAP]

No literal field of black mood could sap
the happiness of so many limps home.


The at-home stewardess' whim of vacuuming
to cover freshman bass lines
to cover—the last tenant up the walk—
berries falling purple and green,
purple and green
on a face.

What was the idea?

Yours: city insufferable.
Wren taking dirt baths in broken glass.
Something like that. I'll ask
when the bird breaks off into the fire escape to talk about late
and you wake up.

I have no
Queen Anne's lace alone at noon
to restore me since
I know some stands out there, safe from me.

My idea: that's good.

When I said I hated robins,

who was walking outside bareheaded?

Someone moving to a new place: a person carrying

the boxes painted red, drawers

that would hush to black as a hand pushed knob

into a right

place.

But when did I say I hated robins?
I love those shocked white rings around the eyes.


Me: stunned by his swing set noise. I see
him and his brothers, running twigs under feathered boats,
loaded with *the secrets of living.*


But birds speak non-English
in starry heads such that really
I can prove their theorems
watching pink skirts go by,
watching Mohawked pizza guys, white Vietnamese sandals go by.


That's the convalescing adolescence: thing.
Another picture taped up next to it: idea of thing.


And a bird, nameless,
alone at night kites himself at hardware white dwarfs,
some guiding star.

# BELONGING

Feeling of home, feeling of home.
Caramel can be pushed to a point of bitterness.
This mind half shell of Jordan almond,
half idea of a spiritual home.
Living in attics for a decade, I looked
down through snow at passersby.
Fingerling potatoes dying in a drawer,
I saw crumbled border trees throw
yellow money at the sky: each metropolis
never trying to catch anyone as he fell.
I really believed better everything's exposed
conglomerate rock, that makeshift showroom tub
barely big enough to stand in but not turn around in.
We could pearl gray snow flung like the dead.
I could soap bar silver without wasting a drop.
Used to be, the historical hysterically renovated
Boston Commons, pink dough heads lining the prow
of a tree ornament, Faneuil Hall
pronounced Daniel full of humid women,
the affluenza professors: was the light wrong?
My bad, bad faith in rivers poured rain
a useless windshield. But now
to lay eyes on straw and beer-colored brick
thread-like gradations of ochre, everything
finished milk gray, a small chip of lilac
sky sliding across each eye. It might be the cold.
I heard of a painter who decided she would do without color—
paint animals without color. Or fruits. Used to be, I'd
understand that decision to waste not even a tube of red
and now I can't take it, can't take the thought
of the actress who'd said
she planned to starve herself to nothing
then rebuild with solid muscle. Each fever
wants to self-swaddle with precision.

This isn't about a lacquered boutique but a for-once
rise-up feeling nothing is missing, the mind
a candy dish with a ridge across the bowl. The feeling
nothing is missing the mind. Eating Red Delicious
apples one after another that had once tasted bitter.
The car driving uselessly a route the shape of a square.
Pale blue arrows on the TomTom a reason for going
off-route. Holding up traffic five hours to throw an ascetic
off a bridge. Trundling between knot and go. Suddenly,
in the right place. I gaze at the absurd alikeness of two
shining pints of water: one bubbled, one still.

## MANIFEST

Slowly, my mother warns the paintings are too *crammés dans le salon*,
too crammed across the walls. Looking is moss that needs space.
The day her class sketched animals at the Jardin des Plantes,
each vein a well-placed filament, graphic and graphite,

she drew, her eye took in neck or back descending, marked it.
They were told, *Copy the animals*, scrape charcoal to paper's bite.
She walked through the salon of creatures listed and stuffed—
straw, sand inside skin, a herd of each kind posed.

Not yet to the year she'd climb a boat, one name
on a list of hundreds and leave all behind save sons, a husband—
she sat, a girl in a museum contemplating small clusters,
animals in twos lined up, their rescues stuck or impossible.

What kind of reverie worked itself in such gray sheets of light
that she looked up and saw her whole class had left?
The slow panic of trying every door. Lights turned low
and knobs pocked where rings and bags had caught.

In this incarcerated calm, her satchel, a tablet in hand while she
waited for a hand to undo the way home: each animal head
cocked back natural—owl, snake, hippo, bear, deer.
Nothing to ply, no second baguette to throw

hungry for fear's sake, silent tuft and glow of closing time.
Silence lit a hat she'd thrown. Eventually her shouts of *Je suis là*,
*I'm here* would solve the mistake. But in a museum of the captured wild,
*If all these animals come alive, I'll be dead*, she thought.

## BONDS

Houdini standing with his hands cuffed, tailored suit, white shirt.
His fall over the cliff. Barrel nailed shut, unseen grimace.
This is the sexiest act. This is the biggest faith.

An escape down waterfall to a middle point; within
this container he doesn't contemplate how wet,
the act flies, tied in the straightjacket, these comprehensible
slots and flaps. His body nestles as it hits the lake.
Counts down the seconds until he can snake-to
his get-up and slide off this nothing-but-restraints.

A yellow parrot—*fringey*, you said, *haphazard*—
paused on a railing over the beach, never moving.
We stared quietly at his colors, his lack of flying away.
I asked the guy reclined beneath the parrot,
*Does that bird belong to you?*

Why does something yellow and green and alive belong here?
And the man shook his head no, pointed to the people
crowded near the waterline. They read magazines,
talked sandwiches, indifferent. The bird stayed and stays,
trusts in his rail and blue lintel of sky.

Houdini pulled twenty needles from his mouth strung on one thread
and a skeptical conjuror explains to today's audience
how Houdini fooled us: he held the needles close together in his mouth,
their eyes aligned and threaded them all at once
using his tongue. The thread was there all along in his mouth.

As if this defuses our wanting.
As if this anything can be explained.

The deer, two deer unconcerned in the shoulder, eat,
open to all the cars that drive past. The speeds
absurd and the shoulders so narrow. The animals
prove that known dangers—cars, crack of twigs,
speed, or blindness—have been mis-identified.

I like the part where your clothes are still on and you
might come around the corner with a coke
and open a door for me. I like the part where
all my misplaced affections all these years now
turn into something I always wanted—
stretched, arms up, blue torso.

When you went onto the theater set and stole a lamp,
iridescent with flowers and bronze filigree,
there stood one less thing to turn on.
One less trick, one less kingly prop.
And that lamp is always in your house, on.

Light blares in as if to take a hostage.
Light tightly held to the walls.
We wish we could cover our eyes, bellowing
at the glare, the idea

of our attachments and supple thoughts illuminated.
This loud and comical *no*,
seeing my finger
on the light switch, *no* to the idea of work,
to the idea of leaving this captivity,
*no* to the idea of finite corners and white.

## IN PRAISE OF HAWTHORNE OVER A PLATE OF GAI TOM KHA

This saffron comes from a field near Singapore, these noodles from New Jersey.
I love my country. Today, I read about Dimmesdale over lunch—

his gorilla-like meltdown on the scaffold—baring to everyone the A
gnawed into his chest by a tooth of remorse. A man across the restaurant

was shouting, *Do you believe in fornication?* to his lunch date.
Getting acquainted. He said, head back, *If it's one of the ten*

*commandments, it must go against human nature.* Like God thought
it up to see how bad we could fail. Hawthorne used to personify

sin—*letters in the shape of figures of men &c.* proceeding along.
Ten thoughts we should shave down to what they really mean.

I peered over at the diners. Were they going to love each other? She looked
trapped in this purple waistcoat, gold buttons for *distance, the words*

*composed by the letters . . . alone distinguishable.* Dismay, I read.
You never bothered to say what the A stood for. Rather,

you said *that close at hand, the figures alone are seen, and not*
*distinguished as letters.* I couldn't hear most of what they said,

but pieces boomed out over the orchids and gold threads
of Thai tablecloth: a mind's light overhead and frayed,

or a light, gleaming snake hanging overhead in
wine dark, promise glowing from its mouth. An honest red

slipping through. The waitress leaned by herself,
no help, one arm out, and the hair long like something lent

you want back. To a painter looking in, glare shifting on glass,
the menagerie of us must have posed mundane, no tableau

like a flushed girl screaming vermillion, a thrown-off letter afloat.

# THE CAKE ROOM

*Dost thou think, because thou art virtuous,*

*there shall be no more cakes and ale?*

Twelfth Night

Marina knows Alluvial Fan. Her God puts glass in the grass. I know Tumulus. My God picks up the bracken and presses it to his cheek, and goes back to drinking bottles of ether after a momentary nap in the dirt. We had never met. Marina born within a month of me. Two moons-in-Scorpio in such proximity. Wow. I said hello expecting a ticking Parisian crocodile. She smiled big. I smiled back. I had written a poem about slip-on basketball shoes: Marina appeared in slip-on basketball shoes. We bought soap. We thought about being international Belgian spies with white Jack Russell Terriers. We read our poems out loud in the cake room. We knew audience. We knew hantavirus and kombu. The Plains Indian with the hatchet reared on us was Scrutiny. I momentarily felt like barfing. She looked worried and asked for a hug.

Afterwards, we shopped for clothes. Marina smiled on the silver and black dress with rhinestone buttons. We agreed on the pleasantness of a necklace with pink balls carved into roses. Soon, I washed my hands in a silver and black river of rhinestone fish deep in Kentucky. Marina lathered pink soaps from the back of a toilet in New York. Marina's Portuguese mother says, *Even the blind chicken gets the corn.* My French mother says, *Little by little the bird makes his nest.* Above her, Marina's ceiling is yellow with crème trim and a chandelier. My ceiling is yellow with no chandelier. The chandelier showing up in one photo and not the other is framing. Of course, we were in the same room at the same time.

## THE BEST PRICE YOU CAN GET

I slept pretty still, then. But,

as if someone had taken a busy pool at noon

and put it next door at midnight, small sounds

un-leaved themselves, one coarse waxy hand at a time:

someone shouted *she's a whore*, ran to his car, and sped away.

The gas can kicked across the street, impromptu soccer,

voices merging and throwing hard bottles into

the thought of a donkey we could visit the next day.

My mother scolded me for something at a store from thirty years ago,

for hiding under the clothes of a carousel rack.

Sun clipped itself at a million angles and widths

to help the fevers go down.

                              Faith, walking

through routines that answer to reality.

Then the neighbors all roared at a joke you or I might have liked

but couldn't hear. And before their fits spilt like candles knocked off,

they streamed into their house, shut it up.

No one uttered a thing about the best price you could get for this.

I didn't look at your sweet lips again. Night held its own.

Pauses and desires grew separate until the minds folded their own sleeves

like laundry and together, or, simultaneously, we all slept.

## RENÉ ET GUY MOQUET

Over grinding subway tracks an uncle rides to work,

pulling down his sleeve to watch a station name go by: Guy Moquet.

The names go by: Tour Eiffel, Montmartre, station names

mean building, mean artists, but the dictionary lists *Guy Moquet,*


*boy gunned down in the street.* Germans occupied the cold:

but one boy takes action—one foot off pavement—and leaps.

My uncle René rides through a subway station all his life,

turning over his wrist to see the time, lifting his eyes:


Guy Moquet, seventeen, fallen in the street, shot

while others begged his life be spared. Before this fame,

he and René had stood on a soccer field, night far off,

keeping their eyes and hopes well-poised. Neither


would ever touch the ball they guarded. Le foot's

grass-stained sepia from that day: a click, a photo

that traps wide-slumped leaves, capturing softness

like dry cloths pulled apart and laid at the feet

of upright boys: pensive, toward, waiting for the ball.

Grown, René rehearses his lines in the amphithéâter, heroic;

and lipsticked actresses recently thinking of sandwiches

look on his acted rage in acted horror. He opens himself up

to night's black trove, well-starred painful luck, a drive

towards old seethings he can later hang on air. He

drives fast on streets where, as boys, he and Guy Moquet stood

for sun and being game. Felled or lame, an uncle rides a train.

In his mind, those boys dissolve to widths of light

whose Paris melts to mere city, its chestnuts nestled

in a paper cone. Their lives split. Eyes shielded by hands.

A ball kicked and dark traveling under its flight.

# BARRACUDA

We've never talked about the boy that drowned
while you were trying to save him from the waves.

And last week in Puerto Rico in water so warm
you weren't sure if you were actually in it,

your friend saw, moved at your browning
face with purpose, screamed at you,

*Look out, a shark*—it was a small four footer. You
weren't scared, used to the ones at home, to *harmless.*

Down the actual block from your house, they say
fear is one's discipline stepped up a notch,

stupidity as a chaser that stands up and ignores
in that shallow water. They say a lot of things but

nothing helps when soft aqua quartz falls all around you.
Standing up in the sand, the truck about to trawl

that perch on stilts that never touches the water.
*That a small shark is harmless.* Except it was

a barracuda. A barracuda. The kind of jaws that
bite, have bitten, and will again bite in two

a massively twitching unsuspecting specimen,
its back half gone. We laugh the ache of a pointless oar

and dangerous mistaken identities for an hour—
videos cued online; bites and heads jerked back.

## COMPASSION FATIGUE

Watching the man with a fractured skull chew buttered toast

hearing the doctor ask why I'm on such a long break

I count off silently how long it will take him to chew the banana, drink milk

knowing how long it will take the aide to sprinkle the other patient with powder

I think about a soldier felling a soldier

and then about a doctor facing that salad of limbs

and someone later complaining about a blown-off knee

to him, like someone complaining about a hair in mashed potatoes

in the meantime, I think of small rabbits huddling in a hutch noses cold

malformed pity mostly a spoon of fear to walk around

I think of eating three plates of stew in my dream

of a complicated piece of cloth trying to be more than what it is

I wish the children could drive themselves to school, skilled as they are

the nurse steamrolling her cousin on the phone:
        *only two beers, God I just hate that for you*

*hate that for you:* the way people break down at the smell of disease

metal beds, marble floor too hard to walk

I consider a reply to *I need, I need*

sympathy like touching one's forehead with paper

now come back to the pine with a notion of yearning

now come back to a fragrant shoulder and bolt

now come back with the fake millstone of observed pain gone

of wanting to be wrapped in gray elastic cloth

wrapped stiff and set down to work in cold wood

pulling necessity taut; no touching down into emotion

bandaging the wound, seeing and spooning ice into the mouth

## VESTED WITH TRUTH

A wind singes a seam. The wind jaywalking. I jaywalking.

Three girls with dachshunds jaywalking. Me fast. An old woman
vested with rage yells, *Do you know what criminal intent is*—
                                   her tears yellow glass over
dim blue flints, the red in her face held to a hot pan.
An old woman needs rest and to shoot off a gun,
                              what July said,
the salts off, her blood a collection of boxes hiding
                             what starts with cock,
crawls along road, and ends with roach. Sun peels her voice. A shock
in green like static through the brain, and slumped:
                 assault, here I shred the notion

of criminal intent. You can't save will suddenly. That sky's been gone
since, as a girl, you saw a bird and wanted feathers for yourself,

or saw a tree when you were a ship, and felt salt in your joints.

# ON THE OCCASION OF YOUR LENDING ME A SHOVEL

The long snowy pause before I said anything.
Sunshine plausible elsewhere, unseen,
I said goodbye, walked into the subway. We'd
been talking about the quality of feeling
a thousand times happier alone. In a dark car
you'd said, *I'm not holding back anymore, I'm just*
*telling it like it is no matter what.* A dark sidewalk
where we saw the soldier in camo walk his python,
his one friend not dead in Iraq. You and I talked
about my blocking the number again—
the block expires every 90 days; you said how great
to banish drama easily, *a good sign, a good sign.*
I barely remember anything about that sadness except it
wiped off my kid-face. And so this out-of-prison sneaking—
I'll be damned to let the past snow itself into this
shoe. In flashes I recall flesh. Down the subway
stairs, I hold the shovel in front of me like a bayonet
edge out, handle high above my head. On the platform,
a handsome dude with a cased cello strapped
to his back. Music and what miscalculated
distraction streamed out, commiseration, hate.
He and I get on the train. He'd gotten an idea,

plunged his hands into side pockets, blank

sheet music pulled out, big headphones on,

started composing a song right there. Love that:

I sit near this hot cello guy and a rogue toddler

tries to kick the shovel out from between

my legs, playing it off as if he can't see this

incredible rusted texture, this destroyed wall.

And to get the car out, to get driving, you've

lent me a shovel. You tell your guy it's too fast. He gets it.

I tell the sweet old lady thanks because she gets it,

she won't make me call back tomorrow to

block the number, I've called a day early and she's

made herself a post-it—do it the next morning.

*The shovels sold out*, the shoveling girl said,

throwing snow away. Winter cannot contain

but maybe better a new poem on a white sheet.

And the enormous what I want, a loud uncalled-for,

the bed covered with coats in case I get cold

in the night, the red help of faces. I stir to get up.

The shovel slams into the cello and the musician

almost smiles but his eyes never leave the page,

never leave that small thing at hand.

# HUNGARIA

To fall down and collect an aspirin
from a hand in the morning. I have the phrase
*I don't want to pretend*, repeating in my head

but with a straight face tell a friend about some date
whose parents hail from Hungaria.

Although a small snowflake crocheted
would make a cheap gift, I'm tired of patterns and kits.

What country is that, really?
*I don't want to pretend.*

Maybe this is the one time a perfectly good person
decided to be someone else. To be false.

*You look old* is no longer a reason to slap on concealer.
We meet one man after another and give report;

how snow grows dense,
a manager that talks to you while walking from

the storefront to the back
carrying an impossibly big machine.

I blame the mother, which is a completely

original thing, you know? Pang.
Pang no longer antecedent to the whim.

## POEM TO MY YOUNGER SELF

Which first seconds full of cymbals, that clean penny intro,
I wished stretched the whole song
but a ragged voice breaks in
with its finite idea, abrupt into sea swarming like leaves.

Don't believe for a minute that similes endure
or that like means anything large scale, (see "like minds").

Like-minded, I've
been stuck with myself, giddy gazes
that ruin a whistled tune. In a decade, your heart may never
fully pump out its sorry.

My heart never fully pumps out its sorry.

## NIGHT AVAILABLE

We pass over a long bridge being

built while we ride it, your favorite

pasture of goats to the side, a picture of goats

up a tree earlier that day, recalled from the web;

birds sew a long thread that spells

red and brown. My hair, too long, decides

in the rearview to look eternal or sage, as if

looming, *you never know what you'll wake to.*

There's no way back from this story

to the goats. A stylist snips and a woman

claims her children three and five are more

animal than human, then pays. I sit,

the stylist combs my hair to a peak. I flash

on a desiccated body, a marble foyer

but don't scream. The stylist pulls my hair down,

cuts it blue wet and straight across. What sweep

what an arena, what happens in imagination:

dead bodies, birds sewing trees, a thought

where you appear as my co-worker scolding

me about my large city of Styrofoam

and glue guns when in real life I rub your arm

often. The goats aren't really up that tree. Scissors

click, hair falls through air. Having received

sophisticated instructions to immediately lie down,

the hair looks flung, starts a wave, incidental

hair of a child whose whole mien says

*almost*. These abstractions grow an impossible lie,

and perfection forms slowly, flopping to one

region of pillow, hair awry like a cow tongue

and lathers. I fall asleep. I keep this to myself:

I asked for dog ears. And this: always claim

there's night available for darting words

that sing *there's some other version you don't see.*

## WAITING

I'm waiting for the eggs to reach room temperature.
I'm not sure if it's better to read all the Flannery O'Connor stories
in a row or one a summer so I have something to live for.

My father used to receive his chocolate out of the Lindt box
and set it on the arm of the sofa
where it stayed through the entire opening of the Christmas presents.

My father used to open his presents with a knife-edge to the Scotch tape
so that the whole piece of paper fell from the gift, not a tear.

Tomorrow the internet will come on in this place and I regret not waiting longer,
so many hours filled with the intent to be lost.

Each man laughs at entirely different things than I would.
I fire them one by one, tell them *sorry.* Stephanie tries not to read
more than four books at a time, young and wise.

How in this confusion can beloved things accumulate?
Not even paintings escape being thought of
and waited for. Slowly,
the thought of this living room
and everyone I love gathering.

Even my cherished dead, alert on this futon. They
party with the living, those daily-called
and the long-departed from my life. Din of dishes. Accents.

A wind heaves, the power line pops.
Outside, a mob sound rises and all I see are people
pouring from their houses with children in cloud-stamped pajamas.

## ACKNOWLEDGEMENTS

*Catch-Up Louisville*: "Hungaria"

*Coconut*: "The Best Price You Can Get"

*Fogged Clarity*: "Setsuko Hara"

*Forklift, Ohio*: "Wabisabi, Nebraska," "Self-Portrait: Looking and Looking Away," "On the Occasion of Your Lending Me a Shovel," and "How do You Define Bliss, Love?"

*Fou Magazine*: "Night Available" and "L'Assemblée Nationale"

*H_ngm_n*: "Je est Un Autre"

*The Kenyon Review*: "Explaining the Sublime"

*MiPoesias*: "French Mother With Tornado Sirens in Background" and "Compassion Fatigue"

*Octopus Magazine*: "Ode to Not Dreaming" and "The Cake Room"

*TYPO*: "Belonging"

*Witness*: "Deer of Los Angeles"

# NOTES

Sincere gratitude for the making of this book and for editorial help go to S. Whitney Holmes, Hanna Andrews, Colleen O'Connor. Thanks for editorial help goes to Hillary Gravendyk, John Drury, Don Bogen, Joanie Mackowski, Adam Clay, Lesley Jenike, Paige Taggart, Kristi Maxwell, Michael Rerick, Matt Hart, Betsy Wheeler, Alice Notley, John Branscum, Thom Southerland. For inspiration and consultation on many deer photos: thank you Mike Nees. Extra special thanks for being poetry-brained to Mathias Svalina. And thanks especially to Harryette Mullen for choosing this book.

Thanks to the University of Cincinnati, the Charles Phelps Taft Foundation, the Juniper Summer Writers Institute, and the Vermont Studio Center for the time and space for the writing of some of these poems.

"Into the Celery Doors" is a collaboration with Ariana-Sophia Kartsonis.

"Setsuko Hara" draws on the life of the eponymously named actress who, after spending years as Japan's leading star, and being nicknamed "The Eternal Virgin," completely withdrew from public life in 1963 to the small village of Kamakura, and has not been interviewed or photographed since.

"[The Procedure Remained Wholly Mysterious to Me]" is a collaboration with Mathias Svalina.

"The Cake Room" is for M.H.

## ABOUT CYNTHIA ARRIEU-KING

Cynthia Arrieu-King was raised in Louisville, Kentucky. She's currently an assistant professor of creative writing at Stockton College. Her book *People are Tiny in Paintings of China* was published by Octopus Books in 2010 and her collaborative chapbook with Ariana-Sophia Kartsonis, *By a Year Lousy with Meteors*, is forthcoming from Dream Horse Press. Her poems and reviews have appeared in *Boston Review*, *Jacket*, and *Witness*. She lives on the East Coast.